W9-AOI-440

MYSTERIES OF THE PAST

BURIED TREASURE

Saviour Pirotta

RAINTREE
STECK-VAUGHN
RSVP PUBLISHERS

A Harcourt Company

Austin   New York
www.raintreesteckvaughn.com

Published by Raintree Steck-Vaughn Publishers, an imprint of Steck-Vaughn Company.

Library of Congress Cataloging-in-Publication Data

Pirotta, Saviour.
    Buried Treasure / Saviour Pirotta
        p.cm. -- (Mysteries of the past)
    Includes bibliographical references (p.).
    ISBN 0-7398-4336-2
    1. Treasure-trove--Juvenile literature. [1. Buried treasure.] I. Title II. Mysteries of the past.

G525 .P525 2001
930.1--dc21

2001019050

Raintree Steck-Vaughn Staff: Marian Bracken, Pam Wells
Project Manager: Richard Johnson

Printed in Hong Kong / China
1 2 3 4 5 6 7 8 9 05 04 03 02 01

Acknowledgments
We wish to thank the following individuals and organizations for their help and assistance and for supplying material in their collections: Ancient Art and Architecture 13 bottom; Art Archive *front cover, back cover bottom left*, 2, 6 bottom, 9, 11, 13 top, 16 bottom, 20 top, 27; Associated Press 24 bottom, 25; C M Dixon *back cover bottom right*, 3 top, 5, 6 top, 7, 26, 29, 30; Corbis 3 bottom (David Muench), 4 top (Gianni Dagli Orti), 14 (Adam Woolfitt), 15 (Bettman) 17 (Reuters NewMedia Inc.), 20 bottom (David Meunch), 21 (Bettmann), 23 (Charles O'Rear), 31 (Burstein Collection). Peter Newark's Pictures 18 top; Pictureworld 8 bottom, 18 bottom; Topham Picturepoint *back cover top*, 1, 4 bottom, 8 top, 10 top, 10 bottom, 16 top, 19, 22 top, 24 top, 28; Werner Forman Archive 12 top, 12 bottom, 22 bottom.
All artwork by Michael Posen.

▼ Find out the story of William Kidd's hidden treasure on page 16.

H.P

LOOK FOR THE TREASURE CHEST

Look for the treasure chest in boxes like this one. Here you will find extra facts, stories, and other interesting information about buried treasure.

▶ This golden belt buckle was just one of the treasures found in Sutton Hoo in England. (See page 10.)

▶ Some say that the Superstition Mountains hide a mine full of gold nuggets. (See page 20.)

CONTENTS

A World of Treasure

The world is full of hidden treasure. It lies buried under the ground, hidden away in secret spots, or locked away in tombs. The treasures are just waiting for someone to find them.

▲ This beautiful sculpture of a bird comes from ancient Syria. It is made of gold, copper, and blue gemstones.

The rulers of early civilizations liked to own lots of gold and jewels. Riches made them feel that they were special. But their wealth often made other people want to steal it. So, the kings and queens hid their treasure, and, when they died, they took their riches with them to their graves.

► Howard Carter opens the coffin of Tutankhamen. He is careful not to destroy any of the treasures that are buried within.

This bull's head is part of a harp found in the city of Ur in Mesopotamia. It is 5,000 years old. (See page 6.)

Not all treasure was buried to hide it. Sometimes it was dropped or lost by mistake. Other times, volcanoes or earthquakes buried whole towns and cities along with their treasures. Pirates often hid their stolen loot, but many got caught and hanged before they could go back and find it. Sometimes buccaneers, or pirates and adventurers, lost the treasure maps that they had drawn to show them where to dig! Most hidden treasure is dug up soon after it is buried. But a lot more is not found and is still hidden to this very day. Who knows who will find it?

THE OLDEST TREASURE

▲ This section of the royal flag of Ur shows a musician playing to people at a feast.

Some of the oldest treasure in the world was found in Ur, an ancient city in Mesopotamia. Today we call this area Iraq. Five thousand years ago, Ur was one of the most important cities in the world. Then it was taken over by enemy armies. They stole its treasures and left the empty city to fall to pieces.

In 1922, an archaeologist named Leonard Woolley decided to search for Ur's long-lost treasures. He worked for almost five years, digging up one grave after another and finding nothing. Finally he decided that the treasure must have been stolen long ago. Then, just as he was about to give up, he hit gold!

▼ The king's guards in Ur carried daggers like these. The dagger cover is made of pure gold.

One day, Woolley found an amazing tomb. Buried in it was one of the queens of Ur. The queen's bones were still in the tomb. There was a headdress that had gold rings, leaves, and flowers. The queen's black wig was covered with gold leaves, too, and these were tipped with lovely orangish-red stones.

There was a wig that was decorated with golden flowers and had a comb still in it. Nearby were golden earrings and huge necklaces made of gold, silver, and beautiful stones. Outside the tomb, Woolley found some writing. He found out that it said "Pu-abi," which was the name of the queen.

A FIELD OF TREASURE

In 1942, an English farmer found treasure buried in his field in Mildenhall, England. There were silver dishes, spoons, bowls, and drinking cups. These items had once belonged to a Christian Roman general named Lupicinus. His family probably buried the treasure in a hurry some time in A.D. 370. Perhaps they were trying to escape from an attack by the Anglo-Saxons, a Germanic people, and could not return to get their belongings.

▶ This ancient Roman silver dish was part of the treasure found at Mildenhall. The face in the center of the dish is of the god Neptune.

▲ Some of Tutankhamen's golden rings were decorated with scarab beetles.

TREASURES OF THE PHARAOHS

The pharaohs (kings) of ancient Egypt were very rich. When they died, they were buried in huge tombs called pyramids. All their treasures were buried with them so they would be just as rich in the next life, too.

Tomb robbers were always breaking into the pyramids to steal the treasures. So the pharaohs started building their tombs in a secret and mysterious place now known as the Valley of the Kings.

▼ Many ancient Egyptian kings were buried in the Valley of the Kings.

Some of the tombs were built high up in the steep rocks where tomb robbers could not get to them. They had many secret paths leading nowhere to keep away robbers. Also the burial chambers were built to look as if they were only half-finished and held no riches. But thieves still found their way in and stole much of the pharaohs' treasures.

One tomb that robbers did not find was that of the Pharaoh Tutankhamen. On November 6, 1922, the archaeologist Howard Carter found a staircase that led down into the sand to a strange door. A second pathway led to another door and to Tutankhamen's tomb. The treasure inside was so rich and beautiful that no one had ever seen anything like it before.

▲ The back of Tutankhamen's throne shows him talking to his wife, Queen Ankhesenamun.

TUTANKHAMEN'S TOMB TREASURE

When Carter went into the great pharaoh's tomb, he found four rooms filled with treasure. There was a golden throne and furniture, model boats, musical instruments, jewelry, and weapons—even a golden chariot that the pharaoh would have been carried around in. In the burial chamber was Tutankhamen's coffin. The king's body was wrapped in bandages dotted with jewels. On his face was a golden mask.

VIKING HOARDS

Not everyone who finds treasure wants to become rich from it. Edith Pretty owned some land in Sutton Hoo, a village in Suffolk, England. She often wondered what was under the great piles of earth in her fields.

In 1938, archaeologists started digging in the smaller piles. They found a few pieces of pottery and some bones. This told them that Mrs. Pretty's fields were once burial grounds that had belonged to the Vikings—pirates who traveled from Scandinavia to Britain in search of treasure.

▲ These jeweled, gold pyramids were once part of a Viking's sword.

BURIED FROM THE BLITZ

Soon after World War II began, Mrs. Pretty's treasures had to be buried again. This time they were put in a secret tunnel under the streets of London. This way, they would not be damaged by wartime bombs.

◀ These gold coins were found at Sutton Hoo. No one knows for sure who their Viking owner was.

A year later, the archaeologists started digging in the biggest pile of all. Soon they had dug up what was once a giant boat. The wood had fallen to pieces, but the ancient nails were still in place, showing what shape the boat had once been. In the middle of the boat was a burial chamber. It was full of amazing treasure from the time of the Vikings.

There were silver dishes, golden jewels, bowls, spoons, a purse full of golden coins, and many other beautiful and expensive things. Mrs. Pretty gave all the treasure of Sutton Hoo to museums. She wanted everyone to be able to enjoy it and to learn more about the Vikings.

This Viking helmet from Sutton Hoo is made of gold and silver. It probably belonged to a powerful warrior.

WHO WAS BURIED IN SUTTON HOO?

There were no bodies left in the ship. But one of the jeweled things found was a scepter, or staff, decorated with jewels. It probably belonged to a king. So maybe he was once buried there. Some of the coins found were made in A.D. 625, the same year that the ruler Raedwald died. Sutton Hoo might be this famous Viking's grave.

GOLDEN CANNONBALLS

Genghis Khan was the first great ruler of the Mongol empire. He lived in the 12th century. With his armies he conquered many lands. As they traveled from place to place, he and his family lived in a yurt, or tent. The tent was covered with stolen treasures—silks, furs, silver bowls, and jewel-covered swords.

▲ This picture shows Genghis Khan fighting his enemies.

In the end, Genghis Khan's empire stretched from China to the Dnieper River in Eastern Europe. Wherever he went, Genghis Khan made the people give up their hidden treasures. Some of the stolen treasure was used to decorate his tent. The rest was hidden away, and much of it has never been seen since.

▶ This model is wearing clothes like those worn by wealthy Mongolian women around the time of Genghis Khan.

▲ This silver cup was found in a Mongolian khan's, or ruler's, tomb. It is about 700 years old.

▼ This model of a Persian chariot is made of pure gold and still shines as if it were new.

During his battles, Genghis Khan sometimes ran out of ammunition to fire from his cannons. Then he would order his soldiers to melt some of his gold and turn it into cannonballs. His enemies never knew they were being attacked with treasure. And many of the golden cannonballs still lie hidden in fields and forests to this very day.

MORE STOLEN TREASURE

In 1877, a load of golden objects was found by the ancient Oxus River, in Afghanistan. Traders and thieves tried to get the treasure across the Khyber Pass and into India. But it ended up in the hands of an important British soldier who gave it to the British Museum. The treasure included jewelry, dishes, and a tiny chariot with four horses. It is about 2,500 years old. The loot had once belonged to the ancient Persians, who were well-known for making beautiful things from gold.

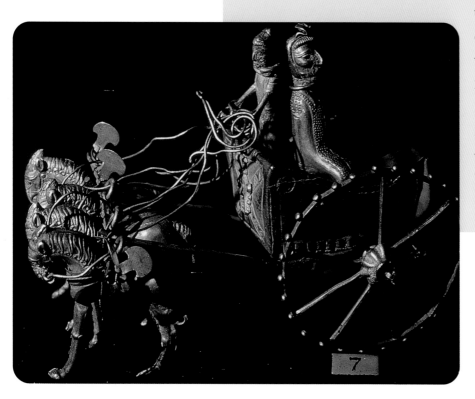

THE GOLDEN CITY

▲ This is the golden model found near Lake Guatavita. It shows a king surrounded by his men.

▼ The mysterious Lake Guatavita lies in Colombia, a country in South America. Who knows what treasures lie hidden in its waters?

Spanish soldiers traveled to Central and South America in the early 1500s. They had heard stories of a city of gold called El Dorado. Some wanted to find this place and take its treasures back to their own country. Many greedy people looked for the city, but none of them found it. Was the legend true?

We now know that the ancient story was not about a city, but a man. He was king of the Muisca people, who lived high in the Andes Mountains near Lake Guatavita. Every year, in a special ceremony, the king was covered in gold dust. He then dived from a boat into the lake to show how much he respected and honored the lake god.

In 1969, two farmers found something really amazing in a cave by Lake Guatavita. It was a golden model of the great king on his boat, with the men who rowed his boat around him. The story of El Dorado seemed to be true after all. Since then people have tried and failed to empty the lake. Who knows what golden treasures still lie in the water where the Muisca dropped them?

GOLD FOR A KING

The English explorer Sir Walter Raleigh tried and failed to find El Dorado for King James I. In 1595, he led a group of travelers to find the famous city in Guiana, in South America.

▲ When Sir Walter Raleigh returned to England without any treasure, the king ordered soldiers to cut his head off!

PIRATE TREASURE

Pirates were the most famous treasure hunters of all. For thousands of years, these sea robbers traveled the world's oceans, attacking any ship they came across. They stole jewels such as pearls, silver, gold, and emeralds. They also took expensive paintings, golden crosses covered with jewels, and all kinds of weapons.

▲ These gold coins were found near a ship wrecked in Uruguay, South America. No one knows whom they belonged to.

Most pirates spent their share of the loot, or stolen treasure, as soon as they got it. But some buried theirs in secret places. The pirate Captain Kidd was said to have hidden his treasure on Gardiners Island off the eastern end of Long Island, New York. He was finally caught and taken to England. To be free again, he offered a huge amount of treasure to the people that kept him prisoner. But everyone thought he was telling a lie to save himself, and the unlucky pirate was hanged in May 1701.

► Captain Kidd watches his pirates dig a hole to hide his treasure.

Some people think that his treasure is still hidden on the island. Others think that he really was lying and had no treasure at all. Perhaps we will never find out what really happened. It is always hard to know who is telling the truth about buried treasure. Everyone wants to find it themselves and they want to stop other people from finding it first!

BLACKBEARD'S TREASURE

The famous pirate Blackbeard is believed to have hidden his treasure somewhere along the East Coast. One possible place was Plum Island, near Orient Point on Long Island, New York. "Only two people know where my treasure is," he liked to say, "me and the Devil. He who lives the longest can keep it all."

◄ Plum Island lies just off the coast of New York. It is named after the many plum trees that grow there.

TREASURE ISLAND

The island of Cocos near Costa Rica is a real treasure island. During the 1600s and 1700s, many pirates used the island as a place to hide. Most of them were trying not to be caught after they had broken the law. William Thompson was a well-known Scottish pirate who was said to have buried treasure there.

▲ Long John Silver is one of the most famous pirates in the world. But he did not really exist. He was a character in the book *Treasure Island*.

▼ The churches on the small island of Gozo in the Mediterranean Sea are said to be full of treasures.

 THE GOLDEN COW OF GOZO

A farmer on the small Mediterranean island of Gozo once found a model of a golden cow in his field. He sold it to a local trader who then hid it. When the person in charge of the island heard about the treasure, he told the trader that he must give it up. But the man said he would not and was sent to prison. He died in jail without telling anyone where the golden cow was hidden. Since then, the people of Gozo have looked for it, but have never been able to find it.

In 1823 rich Spanish families from Lima, in Peru, believed that they were going to be attacked and robbed by local people. They asked Thompson to take them to safety on his ship the *Mary Dear*. Thompson and his men agreed.

But when they saw the great riches belonging to the Spaniards, Thompson's men changed their minds. As soon as they were out to sea, they killed the Spaniards and threw their bodies over the side. Then they sailed to Cocos Island to hide the treasure. Some time later, the pirates were caught and all were hanged except for Thompson who escaped. But he had traveled a long way from his treasures to avoid capture and was too poor to go back and find them.

Over the years many people have tried to find his riches, but nobody has succeeded.

▲ In the past, people liked to take gold nuggets with them on sea journeys. They were easy to carry and hide.

THE DUTCHMEN'S MINE

There is a secret gold mine in the Superstition Mountains of Arizona. The story says that there is so much gold in it that when you tap on the walls, the nuggets just fall into your hands. The Apaches, a Native American tribe, were the first to find the gold in the mountains. They told the Spaniards about the riches when Europeans first visited Arizona in the 1700s.

GOLD RUSH

In 1848, a man named John Marshall found a piece of gold in Sutter's Creek in California. The news caused a wild rush, as people from all over the world hurried to California to find the treasure. This search for gold is still known to this very day as the California Gold Rush.

▲ Gold nuggets like this one are said to be hidden in Dutchmen's Mine in Arizona.

A man searches for gold during the California Gold Rush. He swirls pebbles and water around in a pan. He hopes to find a gold nugget.

◀ The fierce sun makes digging for gold in the Superstition Mountains hard and thirsty work.

Soon, many people were trying to find the mine. The gold hunters fought with one another. The Apaches became angry. The treasure hunters were spoiling their land, so they did everything they could to keep the secret of the mine from them.

Two of the men looking for the gold were German, but the locals thought they were Dutch. They gave the mine its name, Dutchmen's Mine. The Germans did find some gold, but the Apaches then hid the opening to the mine with rocks. Later, an earthquake closed off the mine forever. But, even today, treasure hunters are still looking for the gold. They still dream of great riches.

AFRICAN GOLD

O ne night in 1892, King Lobengula of Matabeleland in Africa went on a secret journey. He carried with him a huge amount of gold, ivory, and diamonds. He knew that the British were going to attack his land, and he wanted to make sure no one stole his riches.

▲ King Lobengula of Matabeleland owned gold, ivory, and diamonds from his own mines.

▶ This golden head was once part of a stool that belonged to an African emperor.

The only people who went with Lobengula were a man called John Jacobs, four chiefs, and some warriors. The warriors buried the treasure, and when they had finished Lobengula told the chiefs to kill them. Now only six people knew where the riches were hidden.

Lobengula died on the run, while hiding from the British. But John Jacobs never forgot Lobengula's treasure. On his deathbed he told a friend named Lloyd Ellis about it.

Ellis traveled all around Matabeleland looking for one of the chiefs who knew where the treasure was buried. Finally, he found an old man who was said to be one of Lobengula's men. But the old chief had lost his memory long before and could not help him. Ellis returned home poor, leaving Lobengula's gold for somebody else to discover. No one has been able to find it yet.

▲ This is what diamonds look like when they are dug out of a mine. Later, they are cut to reveal the beauty of the stone.

THE COAST OF GOLD

West Africa used to be rich in gold. Hundreds of years ago, African gold was sent across the Sahara Desert. There traders gave it to people in return for salt, spices, and perfumes. Soon Portuguese, English, French, and Dutch traders were heading for West Africa to find gold for themselves. They named it "The Gold Coast."

Nazi Loot

▲ This American soldier is inspecting some Italian jewelery from the 1500s. The Nazis had stolen it from Paris, France.

During the 1930s the German dictator, Adolf Hitler, ordered his soldiers to take over Europe. As his troops marched into one country after another, they were told to steal all the art and treasures they could find and send them back to Germany. By 1939, many countries were at war with Germany to try to stop Hitler from taking over Europe.

When the Nazis realized they were losing the war, most of the stolen art treasures were hidden away. Trucks, tanks, and even carts were used to carry the stolen goods up mountain paths to secret salt mines near the village of Alt Ausse, in Austria. There the art treasures were locked in huge caves.

◀ This famous picture of water lilies, by the French artist Claude Monet, was stolen by the Nazis. It was given back to its owner 50 years after World War II.

▲ This is part of a huge hoard of silver stolen by the Nazis. It is being sold after it was found hidden in salt mines in Germany.

ART COLLECTOR GÖRING

Hermann Göring was a very important German soldier. His love of art was even stronger than Hitler's. Whenever his men went to a museum, a church, or an art gallery to steal treasures, Göring always made sure that he kept some treasures for himself.

In France alone, 21,000 paintings were stolen. After the war, thousands of paintings, drawings, models, books, pieces of furniture, and other expensive objects were found in the caves. Before they left to escape back to Germany, the German officers had ordered the Austrian workmen to blow up the mines. But luckily the workmen refused to destroy these amazing treasures. This way, some of the greatest works of art in the world were saved.

FACTS ABOUT BURIED TREASURE

Here are some interesting facts and figures about buried treasure.

Gold

Gold was one of the first metals to be turned into tools and decorations by humans. It is soft and easy to shape. It does not lose its color and it keeps its shine, even when buried for ages. Gold has great value.

▼ This statue from the ancient city of Ur shows a ram in a bush. It was made about 5,000 years ago.

Treasure story

Buried treasure appears in many of the world's myths and legends. In the story the *Arabian Nights*, Aladdin finds a cave full of buried treasure. In another story, Sinbad the sailor falls into a valley full of diamonds and is rescued by a giant bird. In ancient Greek stories, a young prince called Agamedes and his brother build a secret room for a king's treasure. They planned to steal it themselves.

The greatest treasure in the world

Spanish soldiers led by Francisco Pizarro attacked the Inca people of Peru during the 1500s. They put the Inca king in prison and asked for money to set him free. The Incas sent Pizarro huge amounts of gold. It was the greatest treasure the world had ever seen. But Pizarro got tired of waiting for all the gold and left. The Incas left some of the treasure in the jungle, and some of it is still there today.

Treasure Island

The Scottish author Robert Louis Stevenson wrote the most famous book about buried treasure. It is called *Treasure Island,* and some say the author wrote it about the legend of Cocos Island. (See page 18.) Stevenson is thought

to have said that "a man who had not hunted for treasure as a boy was never a child."

Ghostly guardians

According to folklore, ghosts often protect treasures. For example, the ghost of a black hen protects the treasure in an old house in Sussex, England. The hen once attacked a man who was trying to steal the treasure and made him go crazy.

Dragons' pearls

In Persian stories, buried treasure is often looked after by dragons. Kings or brave warriors always try to kill the dragons and steal their treasure. In a Chinese story, a farmer finds a very expensive pearl buried outside his house. When he swallows it by mistake, the farmer turns into a dragon.

The strangest map

The strangest map in the world was drawn by a pirate named Olivier le Vasseur in the 1700s. When he was about to be hanged, le Vasseur threw the map into the crowd and shouted, "my treasures to the person

▲ This golden necklace belonged to Queen Ahhotep Drá Abu-Al Naga in ancient Egypt. It was a present from her sons.

who can find them." But the directions were written so that they were hard to read. No one could figure out what the map said and people are still puzzling over it to this day.

Treasure coast

The coast around the Gulf of Mexico is rich in buried treasure. Many Spanish ships are said to have run into its rocky coastline. A famous pirate named Lafitte is also said to have hidden three treasures in the area, although no one has managed to find them.

WORDS ABOUT BURIED TREASURE

This glossary explains some words used in this book that you might not have seen before.

Afghanistan
(af-GAN-i-stan)
A country in Central Asia. It is east of Iran.

Ammunition
(am-yuh-NISH-uhn)
Items such as bullets and shells that are fired from guns or cannons.

Andes Mountains
(an-dees MOUN-tuhnz)
A long chain of mountains that extends along the west coast of South America.

Apaches
(uh-PA-cheez)
Native Americans of the United States and Northern Mexico.

Archaeologist
(ar-kee-OL-uh-jist)
Someone who studies the past by looking at buried remains of houses, tools, and clothes.

Burial chamber
(BER-ee-uhl CHAYM-bur)
A special place, often underground or deep inside buildings, where people and their belongings are buried.

Central America
(SEN-truhl uh-MER-uh-kuh)
The southern part of North America that is south of Mexico and north of South America.

◄ Tutankhamen's death mask shows him wearing a beard and the headdress of a king.

▶ These silver spoons are from the treasure found in Mildenhall, England. (See page 7.) Their handles look like dolphins. They were made 1,600 years ago when people believed that dolphins brought them good luck.

Chariot (CHA-ree-uht)
A two-wheeled vehicle often pulled by horses.

Dictator
One who holds complete power and crushes those under his or her power.

Gozo
One of the small islands of Malta in the Mediterranean Sea.

Adolf Hitler
(A-dolph HIT-luhr)
An Austrian who ruled Germany in the 1930s. He murdered the people he did not like and tried to take over Europe.

Hoard (hord)
A store of something, such as golden coins or jewels.

Loot (loot)
Treasure that has been stolen from someone.

Mediterranean Sea
(MED-uh-tuh-RANE-nee-uhn see)
A large body of water between Europe and Africa.

Mine
A mine is dug into the ground. Then people can get at the natural deposits that lie in the earth, such as coal or gold.

Mongol (MON-gohl)
A person born in Mongolia, a huge region in Central Asia.

Next life
Many people across the world believe that when they die, they will have another life. This next life may be a different place or time.

Nuggets (NUHG-its)
Lumps of gold, silver, or platinum that are found in the earth.

Pirates (PYE-rits)
Sailors who travel the seas robbing other sailors and stealing ships and boats.

Salt mine (SAWLT mine)
A place where salt can be dug out of the ground.

Scarab (SCA-ruhb)
A big beetle that the ancient Egyptians believed to be sacred.

Scepter (SEP-tur)
A rod held by a ruler. It is a symbol of power.

Tomb (toom)
An area, usually underground, where dead people are buried.

Vikings (VYE-king)
Vikings were pirates from northern Europe who raided many countries.

PROJECTS ON BURIED TREASURE

If you want to find out more about buried treasure, here are some ideas for projects.

LOOKING FOR BURIED TREASURE

It is quite easy and fun to make your own guide to buried treasure in your area. First, find out if there are any local stories about buried treasure. Check in your library to see if it has any information. Don't forget to look at books, magazines, and the Internet. Libraries also keep old local papers that you can look at. Your local tourist office, if you have one, might also have maps and information showing old buildings, castles, or houses. Old buildings often have stories about treasure linked to them.

Once you have decided what stories you are going to have in your guide, you can write or type them up. You can also add any photographs of the sites you are writing about. Then you can bind and decorate your guide.

▲ This golden belt buckle was once used by a Viking warrior in the 1200s.

YOUR OWN TREASURE HUNT

Treasure hunting can be a very good game, especially if it is played in a big area. Deciding how to do it is often as much fun as the game itself. First, tell an adult what you are planning to do.

Then, if he or she is happy for you to do the hunt, decide what the treasure is going to be—a book or a toy perhaps. Put the treasure in a box and close the lid. Choose a good place for your "treasure chest" and hide it. Now draw a map and mark the treasure spot with an X. Then add a few landmarks, like shops, phone booths, or a garage, so that the people on the hunt have an idea of where to go. Now give your friends your map, and see if they can figure out where you have hidden the prize! You can take turns hiding the treasure and drawing the map for each other.

BURIED TREASURE ON THE WEB

If have access to the Internet, you can search for sites about buried treasure. Here are a few buried treasure websites to try:

http://www.activemind.com/Mysterious/- Look through this site for buried treasure mysteries.

http://www.tartans.com - Tells the story of the life of Captain William Kidd.

http://ceres.ca.gov/ceres/calweb/geology/goldrush.html - Tells the story of James Marshall and finding gold at Sutter's Mill.

▶ The jewelry worn by Queen Shubad of Ur was made more than 4,500 years ago. Who knows what other treasures from that time still lie hidden?

INDEX